HOUSES and HOMES

THEODORE ROWLAND-ENTWISTLE

Topics

All the words that appear
in **bold** are explained in the
glossary on page 30.

British Library Cataloguing in Publication Data:

Rowland-Entwistle, Theodore
    Houses and homes. – (Topics)
    1. Dwellings – Juvenile literature
    I. Title   II. Series
    643   TX301

    ISBN 0–85078–592–8

First published in 1985 by
Wayland (Publishers) Ltd
49 Lansdowne Place, Hove
East Sussex BN3 1HF

Phototypeset by
Kalligraphics Ltd, Redhill, Surrey
Printed in Italy by
G. Canale & C.S.p.A., Turin
Bound in the UK by
The Bath Press, Avon

Contents

Small Homes

Home is the place where you live, eat and sleep. When you have been away all day at school or visiting friends, you return home because that is where you keep your clothes and the rest of your possessions. Other members of your family probably share your home.

In Europe, North America and Australia most people live in small houses which are just big enough for one family. The shape and size of a house often depend on where it is. In country areas, where there is plenty of space, people tend to live in **detached** houses, which have land all around them. In towns, large numbers of houses are built in **terraces** or rows, joined on to one another. In Britain **semi-detached**

Terraced houses are usually found in the industrial areas of large cities.

Semi-detached houses in the north of England.

houses are built in pairs, sharing one wall. They are cheaper to build and are warmer than detached houses.

The number of **storeys** in a house depends on how much land is available. Town houses usually have several storeys, so that they take up the least possible amount of land. A **bungalow** has only one storey, although there is often an extra room in the roof. Bungalows are built where there is plenty of land available.

Houses are often built for special purposes. A farmhouse provides a home for a farmer, his family and possibly some of his workers. There are usually

Because land is expensive in cities, many people live in tall blocks of flats.

cowsheds and stables attached to the farmhouse. Houses for elderly people are designed to be easy to look after, with few stairs to climb.

In crowded cities many people live in big blocks of flats or apartments. In the 1980s many tall blocks were pulled down, even though they were quite new, because people discovered that they are very lonely places to live. There are no passers-by to chat with and nowhere close by for children to play.

Most houses in developed countries such as Britain and the United States have a supply of piped water and electricity, and quite a number of them have a gas supply as well. Their toilets and baths are connected to a drainage system. But only 150 years ago few houses had water or proper drains. There was no electricity supply, although some homes had gas. Country cottages in particular were sometimes very unhealthy places. A family of ten or more might share just one large room with chickens, the family cow and other animals. Even today, many people around the world have to live in such primitive and unpleasant conditions.

Living standards are still very low in many parts of the world.

Many houses built in towns, especially during the **Industrial Revolution**, were also unhealthy places. There were not enough houses for the great numbers of people who came to the towns to find work and those there were soon became overcrowded, damp and dirty. Some governments are now having these **slums** pulled down and replaced by more comfortable and sanitary homes.

These slums in Scotland will soon be pulled down.

People tend to build homes from materials that they can find easily, such as wood or stone. The kind of shelter they make depends on their surroundings.

The earliest houses were built of timber; people used to make a wooden frame and fill the spaces in between with wattle, a sort of basketwork woven from thin, flexible branches. They smeared clay over the wattle to form an airtight wall. Some old houses built this way still survive in Europe.

The pioneers in North America used to build log cabins. They laid logs one on top of another and then filled the gaps between the logs with clay.

An old log cabin in North America.

These Egyptian builders are using mud bricks.

In the dry countries of the Middle East, people used to shape clay or mud into bricks which were left in the sun to bake hard. Most homes were built with these mud bricks. Only palaces and temples were built of stone. But if mud bricks become very wet, they crumble. Builders later found out how to make **kilns** to bake the bricks even harder and this is the method they use today. Kiln-baked bricks last for hundreds of years. Sun-dried bricks are known as **adobe** (pronounced ad-oh-bee) in North America.

10

Cement is a very important building material. It is a grey powder made by burning limestone, chalk and clay in a kiln. Cement powder mixed with water dries as hard as rock, so it is used to hold bricks together. Cement mixed with sand and small stones forms concrete. Many tall modern blocks of flats are built of concrete, reinforced with steel rods on a frame of steel girders.

Most modern blocks of offices and flats are built of steel and concrete.

Large Homes

Large houses, built for rich and famous people, cost a lot of money to construct and look after. A great many survive from the past, especially in Europe. They are called 'stately homes' in Britain and 'châteaux' in France. Today many owners of stately homes open their houses to the public. The money people pay to look at the beautiful rooms and furniture helps to pay for their upkeep.

As many as forty people could live in this French château at any one time.

The White House in Washington D.C.

The most important large houses were the palaces of kings and queens. Royal palaces served as government headquarters as well as the ruler's home. Buckingham Palace is still the home of a reigning monarch. It contains the private apartments of Queen Elizabeth II, magnificent rooms used for state banquets and offices and homes for members of the Queen's staff.

The White House in Washington D.C. serves as the official residence of the President of the United States and as his office. It is a palace in all but name.

13

Many of the oldest big homes were castles. They were homes for their owners as well as fortresses. In time of war all the people who lived close to the castle moved inside its mighty walls for safety. Castles are no longer needed to protect villagers from attack, but several remain as homes.

A large house was often home for large numbers of people. Besides the owner, his wife and children,

The ruins of Harlech Castle in Wales.

there might be several more distant relations living in it, in addition to all the servants needed to keep it in order.

Although these big houses were beautiful to look at, they were not easy to live in. They were cold and draughty in winter. Logs had to be hauled indoors to be burned in the huge, cavernous fireplaces. The kitchen might be a long way from the dining room, so that the servants had to run quickly down stone passages to serve the platters of food to the diners before it got cold.

Nowadays many large houses have been divided up to make separate homes for several families, or they have been turned into offices, schools or hotels.

The huge kitchen and fireplace of an English castle.

Homes in Cold Places

Homes in cold places have to have thick walls to keep the cold out and the heat in. In places where a lot of rain or snow falls, the roofs slope so that water can run off easily. Deep, overhanging **eaves** make sure that melting snow drips clear of the walls.

The Eskimos of Canada and the Lapps of northern Scandinavia often built their houses of turf. These 'sod houses' were built close to the ground to shield them from the weather. They were made of a framework of timber or whale bones, covered with turf. Even today some people live in turf houses.

These sod houses provide shelter for the Lapps against the wind and snow of northern Norway.

An Eskimo igloo in Canada.

Eskimos move out onto the ice to hunt for seals when the sea freezes over in winter. They build temporary **igloos**, which are dome-shaped huts made of blocks of frozen snow. These snow houses, heated by lamps burning seal or whale oil, are surprisingly warm. For the rest of the year most Eskimos now live in timber houses.

Open fires in the centre of a room are still found in some areas of the world.

Heating is very important in cold places. In ancient times people used to build a fire in the middle of the main room of the house – which was often the only room. The smoke rose up and escaped through holes in the roof, turning the timbers black as it did so. It was not until about 900 years ago that people began building stone or brick chimneys and fireplaces against a wall of the house.

Central heating was invented by the Romans about 2,000 years ago. Instead of burning small fires in each room, they used one big fire to heat water or air which circulated in pipes or ducts throughout the whole house.

These solar panels use the Sun's energy to provide heating and hot water.

Solar-powered houses rely on the heat of the Sun to provide warmth, hot water and lighting. Solar panels, made up of fine tubes, are placed on the roof facing the Sun. The Sun's rays heat the water that flows through the tubes and collects in a hot-water tank. **Solar cells**, like those used in spacecraft, convert the Sun's heat into electricity. This electrical power can then be stored in batteries to be used when the Sun is not shining. Scientists believe that solar power systems in the home will become widespread by the year 2000.

Homes in Warm Places

People who live in hot countries need much less shelter than those who live in cooler places. They can do many of their household jobs, such as preparing and cooking meals, out of doors.

The Bushmen of the Kalahari Desert, in south-western Africa, move from place to place hunting animals for food. They make camp at water-holes. At these water-holes they find all they need to build **skerms**, simple huts made from a framework of thin branches covered with long, dry grass stems. It takes less than an hour to build a skerm, which is a job for the women of the tribe.

A Bushman's skerm in the Kalahari Desert.

Tribesmen of New Guinea build their villages in forest clearings. Their houses have a bamboo floor raised on stilts above the ground to keep out animals. The roofs are made of grass or palm leaves and the walls of bamboo, bark, or woven matting. Tribespeople in many parts of Africa, Asia and Latin America make similar huts.

A grass-roofed house being built in Sudan.

Fishermen's huts in Malaysia.

Further north, in the Mediterranean countries, houses are often built around a courtyard. Their outer walls shield the courtyard from the Sun's rays, keeping it cool even in summer.

Houses that are built near lakes and rivers may be flooded if the water rises after heavy rain, so they are raised on stilts well above the water level. Ladders lead up to the entrance. At the Tonle Sap, a big lake in Kampuchea, fishermen live over the water in temporary huts on stilts. The huts have to be taken down and moved when the lake floods every year.

These children will spend most of their lives on the waters of Hong Kong harbour.

Thousands of people in Asia live in houseboats. They can be seen along Chinese rivers and in the busy harbours of eastern Asia. In these 'floating towns', the 'shopkeepers' paddle their small boats from one houseboat to another, selling their goods.

However, modern city development in hot countries is very much like that elsewhere. In 1960, Abu Dhabi in the Persian Gulf was a quiet little fishing village of single-storey, flat-roofed houses. But when oil was discovered in the area Abu Dhabi quickly grew into an important modern city. Now concrete tower blocks house most of the people and Abu Dhabi looks much like any other large city.

Homes with a Difference

Stone Age people lived in caves at least 500,000 years ago. Deep inside the ground, caves stay at about the same temperature all the year round, whatever the weather is like outside. Even today some people still have cave homes with rough stone walls. Thousands of gypsies live in caves in the hills of the Sierra Nevada in southern Spain. Caves in the Loire Valley of France have been turned into smart, modern homes. The inside walls are smooth and flat like those in a house. These caves have running water and television.

These modern homes are built into the side of a cliff.

About a thousand years ago a group of Pueblo Indians built their homes along the cliff faces of the Mesa Verde in the south-western U.S.A. Some of the houses perched on ledges against the cliffs and others were inside the mouths of huge caves.

The Ma'dan, the Marsh Arabs of southern Iraq, live in huge tunnel-like houses made of reeds which grow in the marshes. Some of the houses are built on islands, others sit on artificial islands made of enormous reed mats.

Ma'dan children outside their home, which is made entirely of reeds.

The Uru Indians who live among the reed beds of Lake Titicaca, on the borders of Bolivia and Peru, also build reed homes on artificial islands, but their huts have straight walls and sloping roofs.

In some places people live in communities, not in separate houses for each family. The Batak people of Indonesia build houses in which whole clans, or groups of relatives, live together. Sometimes a Batak village will consist of just one long house, in which everything is shared.

Traditional Batak houses in Sumatra.

In Israel people work together on **kibbutzim**, which are communal farms. Single workers and families share a large kitchen and dining rooms. Grown-up people have separate rooms or apartments, but all except the youngest children are brought up together in a children's house close by. After work the parents are free to play with their children.

Not everybody is able to live in one place all the time. **Nomads** wander from one area to another. In parts of Asia and Africa nomads have to move about to find enough grass for their large flocks of animals

A nomad camp in the western Sahara Desert.

to feed on. They need mobile homes. The simplest form of mobile home is a tent. Arab and Berber nomads in the Middle East and North Africa use fabric tents woven from goats' hair. The people of Mongolia make circular **yurts**, which are folding frames of wood covered with felt. The Plains Indians of North America made their **tepees** by covering wooden poles with buffalo skins.

Mongolian tribesmen building the wooden frame of a yurt.

Many gypsies now live in luxurious, modern caravans like this one.

More substantial mobile homes come in the form of covered wagons running on wheels and drawn by horses or cars. Gypsies have lived in brightly painted caravans for hundreds of years. A modern caravan may have several rooms in it, including a kitchen, toilet and shower. Smaller caravans can be towed by car to remote areas to be used as mobile holiday homes; larger caravans are often permanently parked on sites where they can be connected to water and electricity supplies.

Glossary

Adobe Bricks made by drying mud in the sun.

Bungalow A small house with only one storey.

Detached Detached houses are surrounded by open space and are not joined on to any other houses.

Eaves The part of a roof projecting beyond the walls.

Igloos Dome-shaped huts built by Eskimos out of blocks of frozen snow.

Industrial Revolution The change-over from doing all work by hand to using machines. It began in the 1700s and is still continuing.

Kibbutzim Israeli communal farms, on which all the workers cook, eat and live together.

Kiln A large oven for baking pottery and bricks to make them hard.

Nomads People who move from place to place in search of food and water for themselves and their animals.

Semi-detached A semi-detached house is joined to another house on one side only.

Skerms Temporary huts made by the Bushmen of southern Africa out of branches and dried grass.

Slum Housing in poor condition, often with no proper water supply, drainage or electricity.

Solar cell A thin layer of treated silicon which acts as a battery when light strikes it.

Solar power The power of the Sun's rays.

Storeys Storeys are the different levels or floors in a building. Most modern houses have two storeys.

Tepees Tents that were made by North American Plains Indians by covering wooden poles with buffalo skins.

Terraces Rows of houses in which each house is joined to those on either side of it.

Yurts Mongolian tents made from wooden frames covered with felt.

Books to Read

Houses and Homes by Carolyn Cocke (Macdonald Educational, 1976)

Houses by R.J. Unstead (A. & C. Black, 1972)

The Truth about Cottages by John Woodforde (Routledge and Kegan Paul, 1969)

A History of Building Materials by Norman Davey (Phoenix House, 1961)

A History of Everyday Things in England by Marjorie and C. H. B. Quennell (Volumes I-IV) and S. E. Ellacott (Volume V) (B. T. Batsford, 1918–1968)

Index

Picture acknowledgements

The pictures in this book were supplied by: Camerapix Hutchison Library *front cover*, 8, 10, 18, 20, 24, 25, 28; Topham 4, 12, 16, 19, 22, 23, 29; Bruce Coleman Ltd 6 (Eric Crichton), 7 (Chris Bonington), 9 (Leonard Lee Rue), 13 (Norman Tomalin), 14 (Geoff Doré), 21 (Adrian Deere-Jones), 26 (Alain Compost), 27 (Charles Henneghien); Zefa 11, 17; Barratt Homes 5. The picture on page 15 is British Crown Copyright, reproduced with permission of the Controller of Her Britannic Majesty's Stationery Office.